American Flag

Aaron Carr

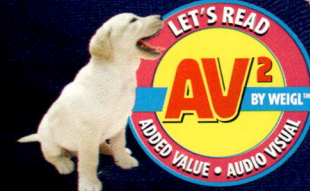

www.av2books.com

AV² provides enriched content that supplements and complements this book. Weigl's AV² books strive to create inspired learning and engage young minds in a total learning experience.

Your AV² Media Enhanced books come alive with...

Audio
Listen to sections of the book read aloud.

Video
Watch informative video clips.

Embedded Weblinks
Gain additional information for research.

Try This!
Complete activities and hands-on experiments.

Key Words
Study vocabulary, and complete a matching word activity.

Quizzes
Test your knowledge.

Slide Show
View images and captions, and prepare a presentation.

... and much, much more!

Go to www.av2books.com, and enter this book's unique code.

BOOK CODE

N288363

AV² by Weigl brings you media enhanced books that support active learning.

Published by AV² by Weigl
350 5th Avenue, 59th Floor New York, NY 10118
Website: www.av2books.com   www.weigl.com

Copyright ©2014 AV² by Weigl
All rights reserved. No part of this publication may be reproduced, stored in a retrieval system, or transmitted in any form or by any means, electronic, mechanical, photocopying, recording, or otherwise, without the prior written permission of the publisher.

Library of Congress Cataloging-in-Publication Data
Carr, Aaron.
   American flag / Aaron Carr.
        p. cm. -- (American icons)
   ISBN 978-1-62127-203-8 (hardcover : alk. paper) -- ISBN 978-1-62127-207-6 (softcover : alk. paper)
   1. Flags--United States--Juvenile literature. I. Title.
   CR113.C375 2014
   929.9'20973--dc23
                                                   2012044670

Printed in the United States of America in North Mankato, Minnesota
1 2 3 4 5 6 7 8 9 0   16 15 14 13 12

122012
WEP301112

Senior Editor: Aaron Carr
Designer: Mandy Christiansen

Every reasonable effort has been made to trace ownership and to obtain permission to reprint copyright material. The publishers would be pleased to have any errors or omissions brought to their attention so that they may be corrected in subsequent printings.

Weigl acknowledges Getty Images as the primary image supplier for this title.

CONTENTS

2 AV² Book Code
4 What is the American Flag?
7 A National Symbol
8 The First Flag
11 Counting the States
12 Choosing the Colors
15 The Flag Code
16 Star Spangled Banner
19 The Pledge
20 The American Flag Today
22 American Flag Facts
24 Key Words/Log on to www.av2books.com

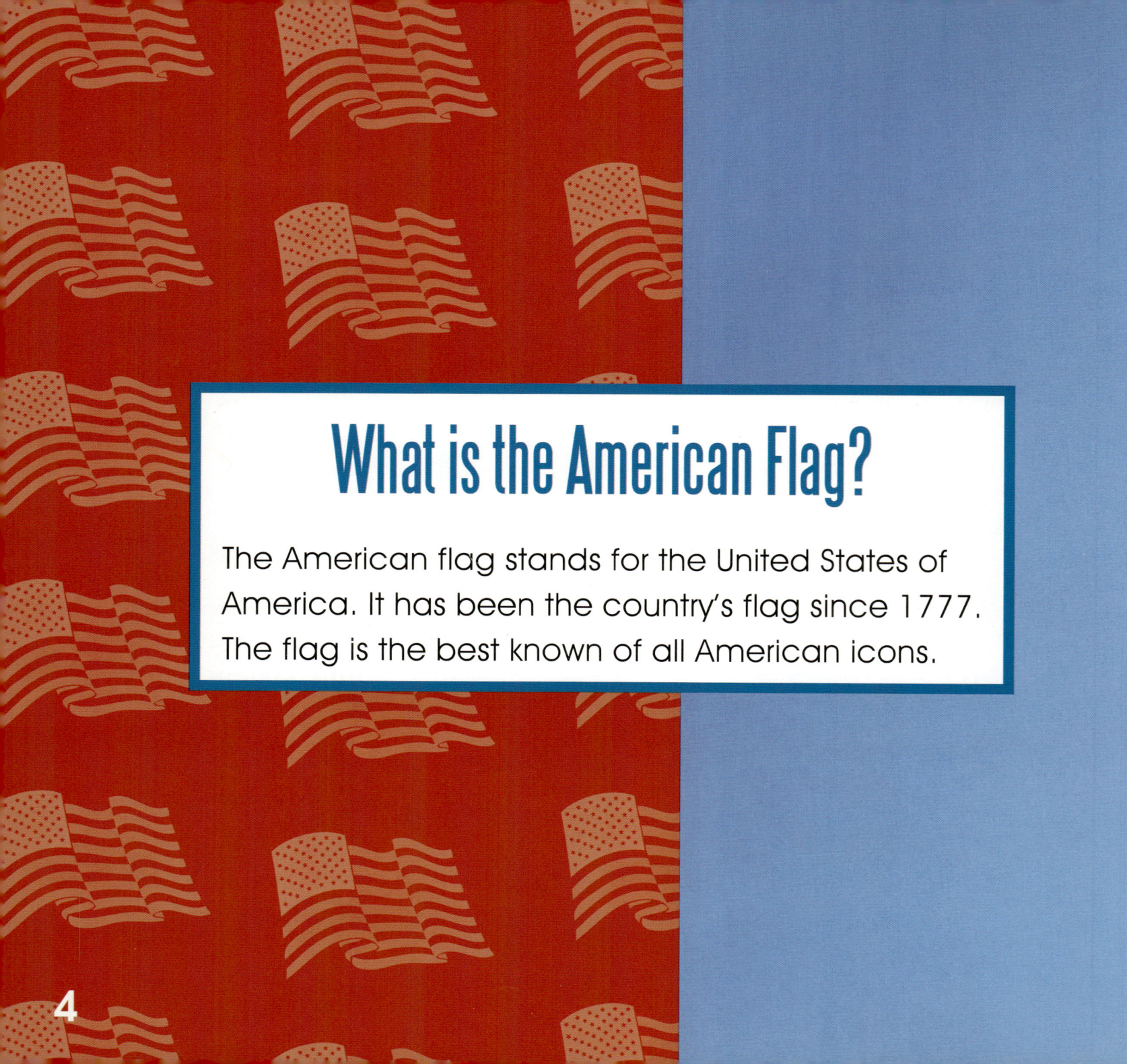

What is the American Flag?

The American flag stands for the United States of America. It has been the country's flag since 1777. The flag is the best known of all American icons.

A National Symbol

The United States had to fight for its freedom from Great Britain. The flag became a symbol of the United States and its freedom.

The First Flag

The American flag has gone through many changes. The first flag only had 13 stars. Today, there are 50 stars on the flag.

Counting the States

The first flag had one star and one stripe for each state in the Union. More stars were added when new states joined the country.

Choosing the Colors

The American flag is red, white, and blue. Each of these colors has a special meaning.

The Flag Code

There are rules for how to treat the flag. These rules are called the flag code. The code says that a flag flown at night must have light shining on it.

Star Spangled Banner

The American flag is sometimes called the Star Spangled Banner. This is the name of a poem written almost 200 years ago. This poem later became the American national anthem.

The Pledge

Many Americans feel proud when they look at the flag. They may say a pledge to show they love their country. This is called the Pledge of Allegiance.

The American Flag Today

Today, the American flag has 50 stars and 13 stripes. There are seven red stripes and six white stripes. The stars each have five points.

AMERICAN FLAG FACTS

These pages provide detailed information that expands on the interesting facts found in the book. These pages are intended to be used by adults to help young readers round out their knowledge of each national symbol featured in the *American Icons* series.

Pages 4–5

What is the American Flag? The first official American Flag was approved by Congress on June 14, 1777. Since then, the flag has become the best-known symbol of the country. Over the past 200 years, the number of stars and stripes on the flag has changed, but the basic design has remained the same.

Pages 6–7

A National Symbol During the early years of its history, the United States had to defend its freedom in two wars—the American Revolution and the War of 1812. Both wars were fought against Great Britain. During this time, the flag became a symbol of independence from Great Britain and freedom for all people.

Pages 8–9

The First Flag The first official American flag had 13 stars and 13 stripes. This stood for the 13 states that first formed the country. There were no rules for arranging the stars on the flag. This led to versions of the flag with rows of stars and another with the stars in a circle. The flag with the stars in a circle is called the Betsy Ross flag, but it was actually designed by Congressman Francis Hopkinson.

Pages 10–11

Counting the States In 1795, two stars and stripes were added to the flag when Kentucky and Vermont joined the Union. The 15-striped flag was the official American flag until 1818, when Congress decided that adding a new stripe for every state was not practical. It was decided that the flag would have 13 stripes. Only a star would be added for each new state to join the Union. Each star on the flag represents one of the states that makes up the country.

Pages 12–13

Choosing Colors When the flag was created, the colors did not have specific meanings. Years later, when Charles Thomson presented the Great Seal of the United States to Congress, he proposed meanings for the colors. Thomson suggested that white would represent purity and innocence, red would stand for valor and hardiness, and blue would symbolize vigilance, justice, and perseverance. These meanings have become associated with the flag as well.

Pages 14–15

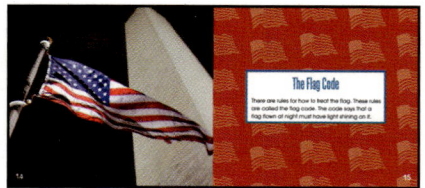

The Flag Code The United States Flag Code outlines many rules for the proper care and treatment of the American flag. These rules are federal laws. Rules state that the flag should never be dipped, or lowered, to any person or thing; the flag should not be used for clothing; and the flag should not touch the ground.

Pages 16–17

Star Spangled Banner On September 13, 1814, Francis Scott Key saw the British attack Fort McHenry in Baltimore, Maryland. The next morning, he noticed the American flag was still flying above the fort. This inspired Key to write a poem called "The Star Spangled Banner," which later became the United States national anthem.

Pages 18–19

The Pledge The Pledge of Allegiance is a statement of loyalty to the United States. It is often spoken by schoolchildren and government officials. The pledge was first written by Francis Bellamy. In 1892, it was sent to schools across the country. The words of the pledge changed over the years, but it has been the same since 1954.

Pages 20–21

The American Flag Today The American flag underwent its most recent change on July 4, 1960, when Hawai'i was added as the 50th state. The flag has remained unchanged since. The 50 stars are arranged in rows that alternate between five and six stars on each line. From 1777 to today, there have been 27 versions of the American flag.

KEY WORDS

Research has shown that as much as 65 percent of all written material published in English is made up of 300 words. These 300 words cannot be taught using pictures or learned by sounding them out. They must be recognized by sight. This book contains 55 common sight words to help young readers improve their reading fluency and comprehension. This book also teaches young readers several important content words, such as nouns. These words are paired with pictures to aid in learning and improve understanding.

Page	Sight Words First Appearance
4	all, American, been, country, for, has, is, it, of, the, what
7	a, and, from, had, its, to
8	are, changes, first, many, on, only, there, through
11	each, in, more, new, one, state, were, when
12	these, white
15	at, have, how, light, must, night, says, that
16	almost, later, name, sometimes, this, years
19	look, may, show, their, they
20	points

Page	Content Words First Appearance
4	flag, icons, United States
7	freedom, Great Britain, symbol
8	stars
11	stripe, Union
12	colors, meaning
15	code, rules
16	banner, national anthem, poem
19	Pledge of Allegiance, proud

Check out www.av2books.com for activities, videos, audio clips, and more!

 Go to www.av2books.com.

 Enter book code.   N 2 8 8 3 6 3

 Fuel your imagination online!

www.av2books.com

4-19-15